Castles & Fortresses

Coloring Book

Gothic Architecture, Fairy Tale Castles,
Medieval Palaces - For Teenagers & Adults

Rachel Mintz

Copyright © 2018 Palm Tree Publishing - All rights reserved.
No part of this publication may be reproduced, distributed, or transmitted in any form or by any means, including photocopying, recording, or other electronic or mechanical methods, without the prior written permission of the publisher, except in the case of brief quotations embodied in critical reviews and certain other noncommercial uses permitted by copyright law.

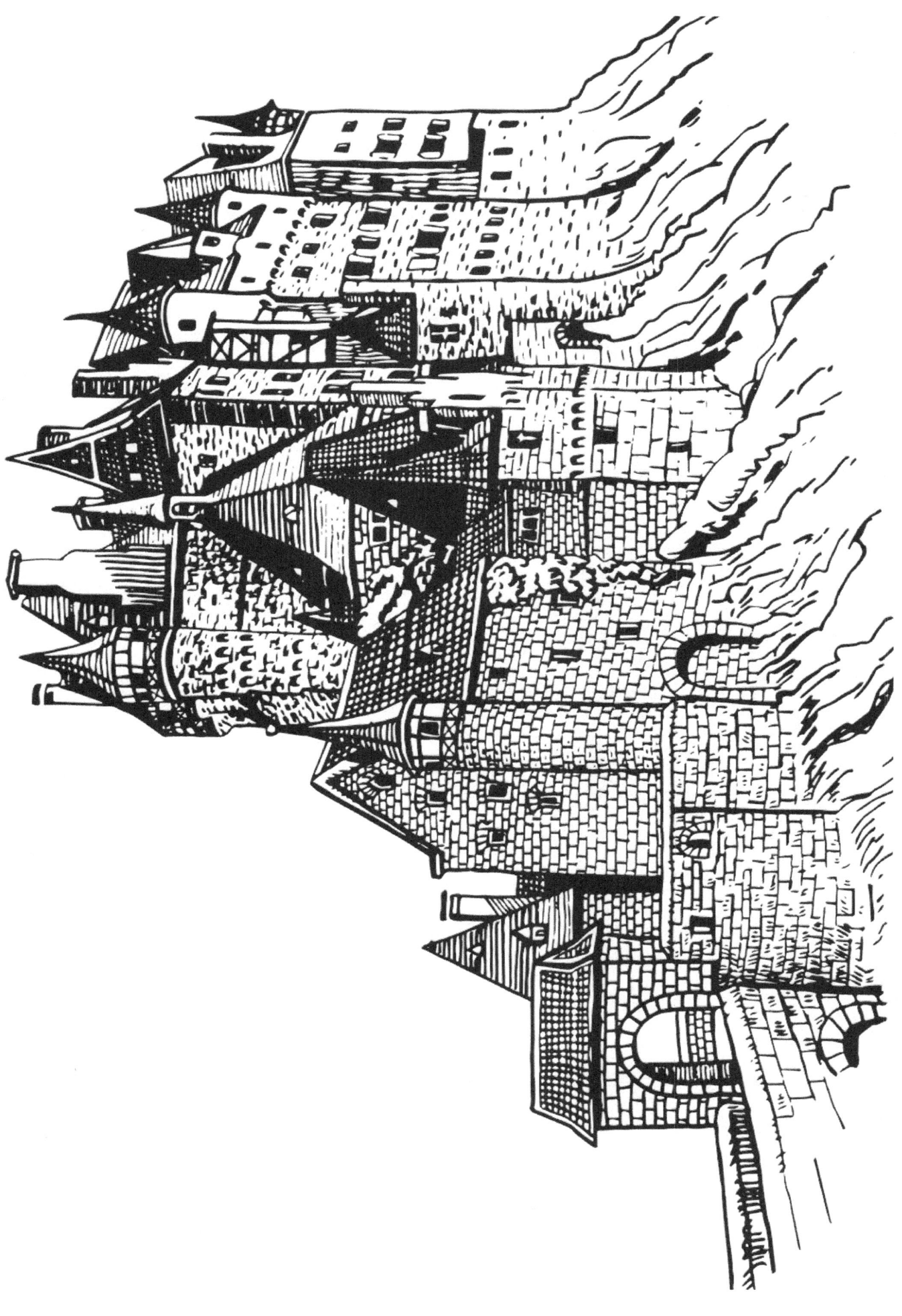

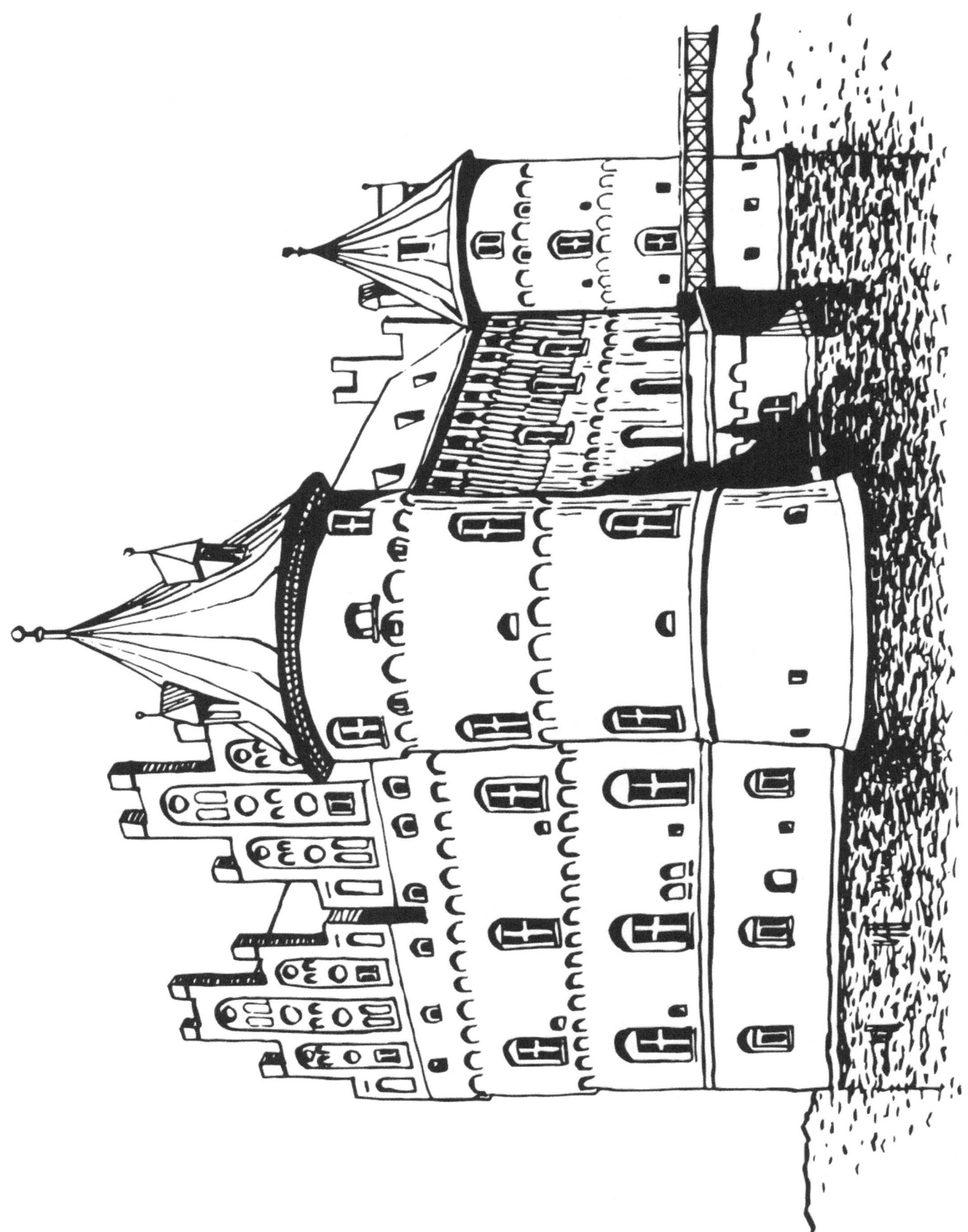

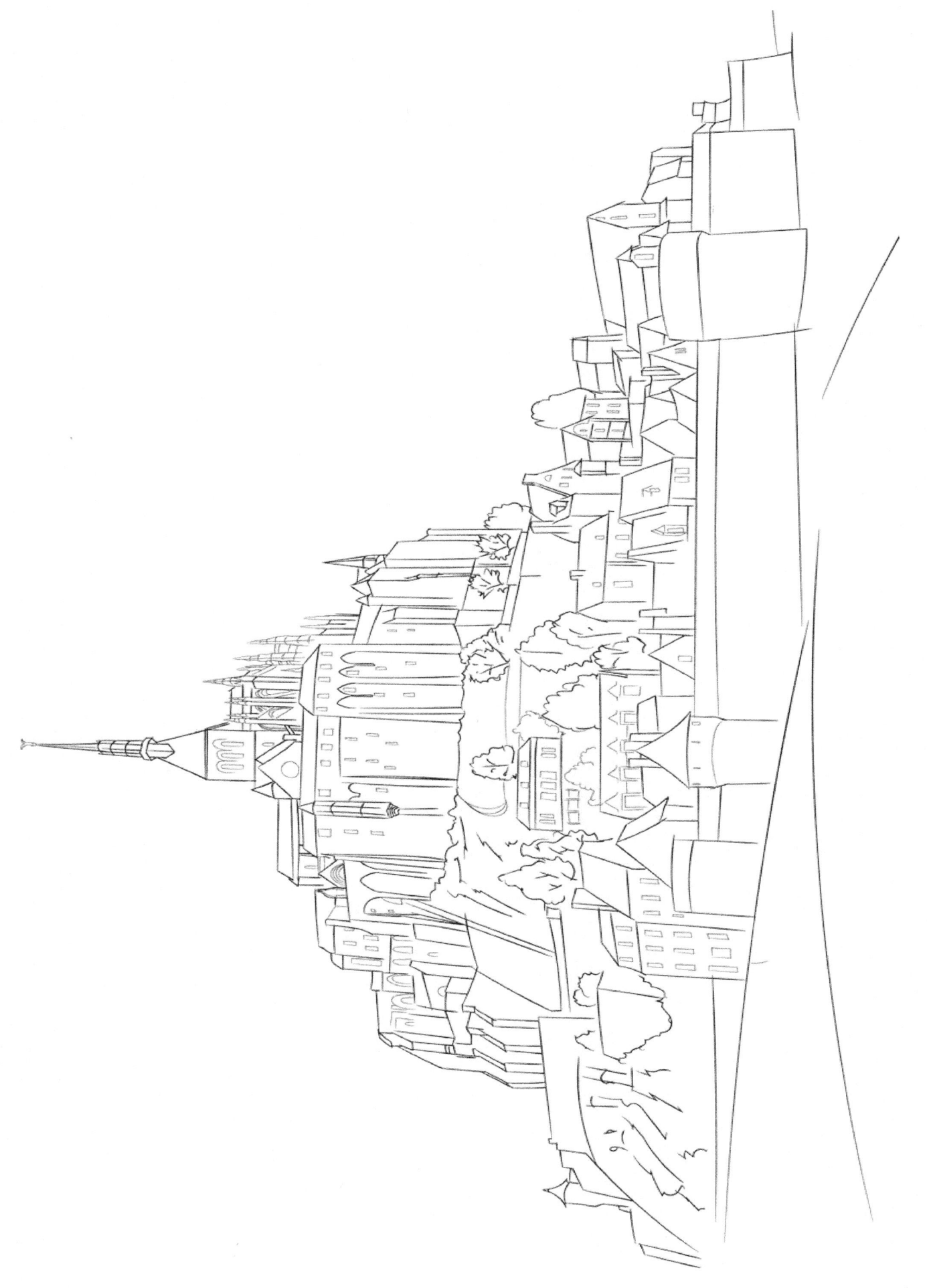

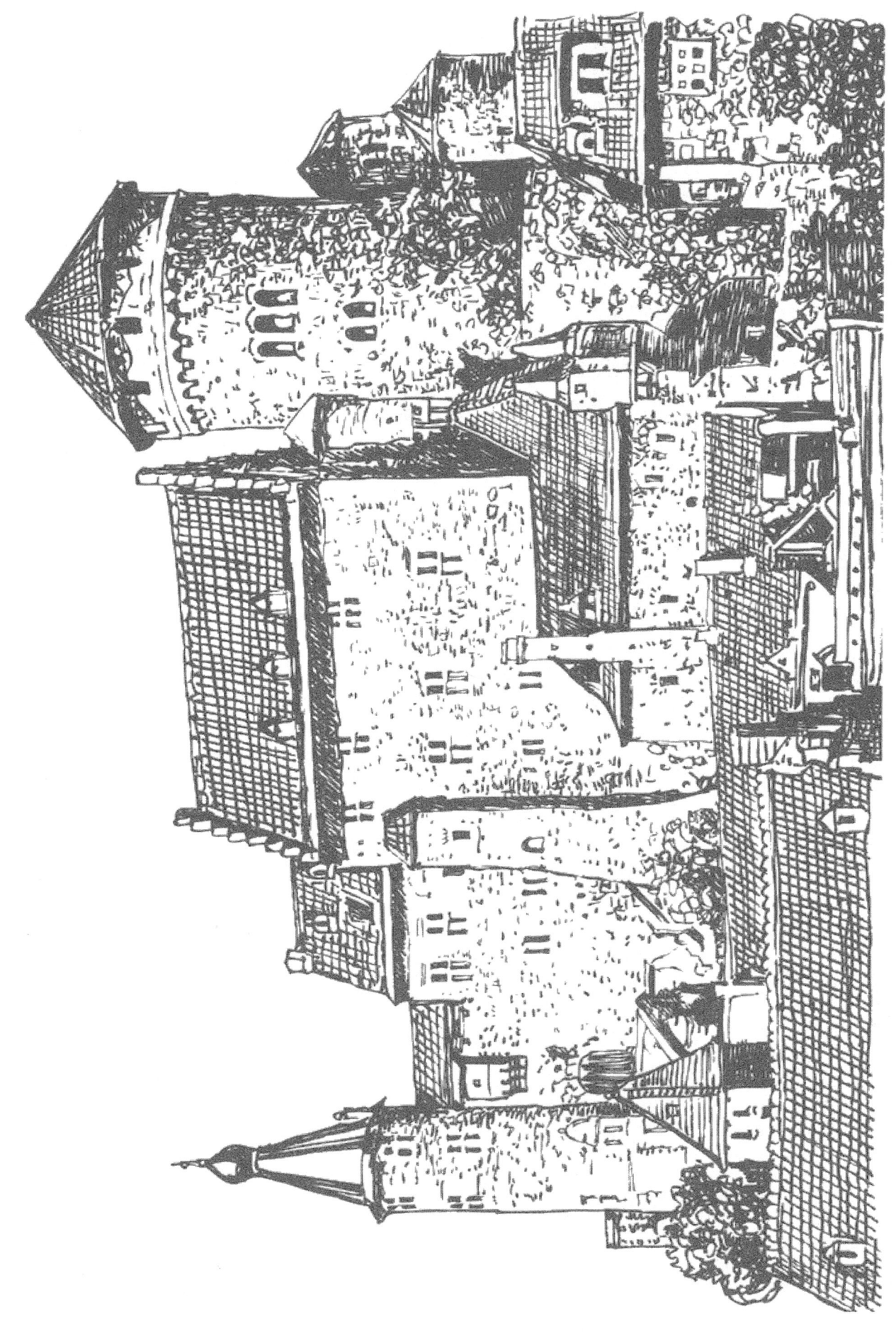

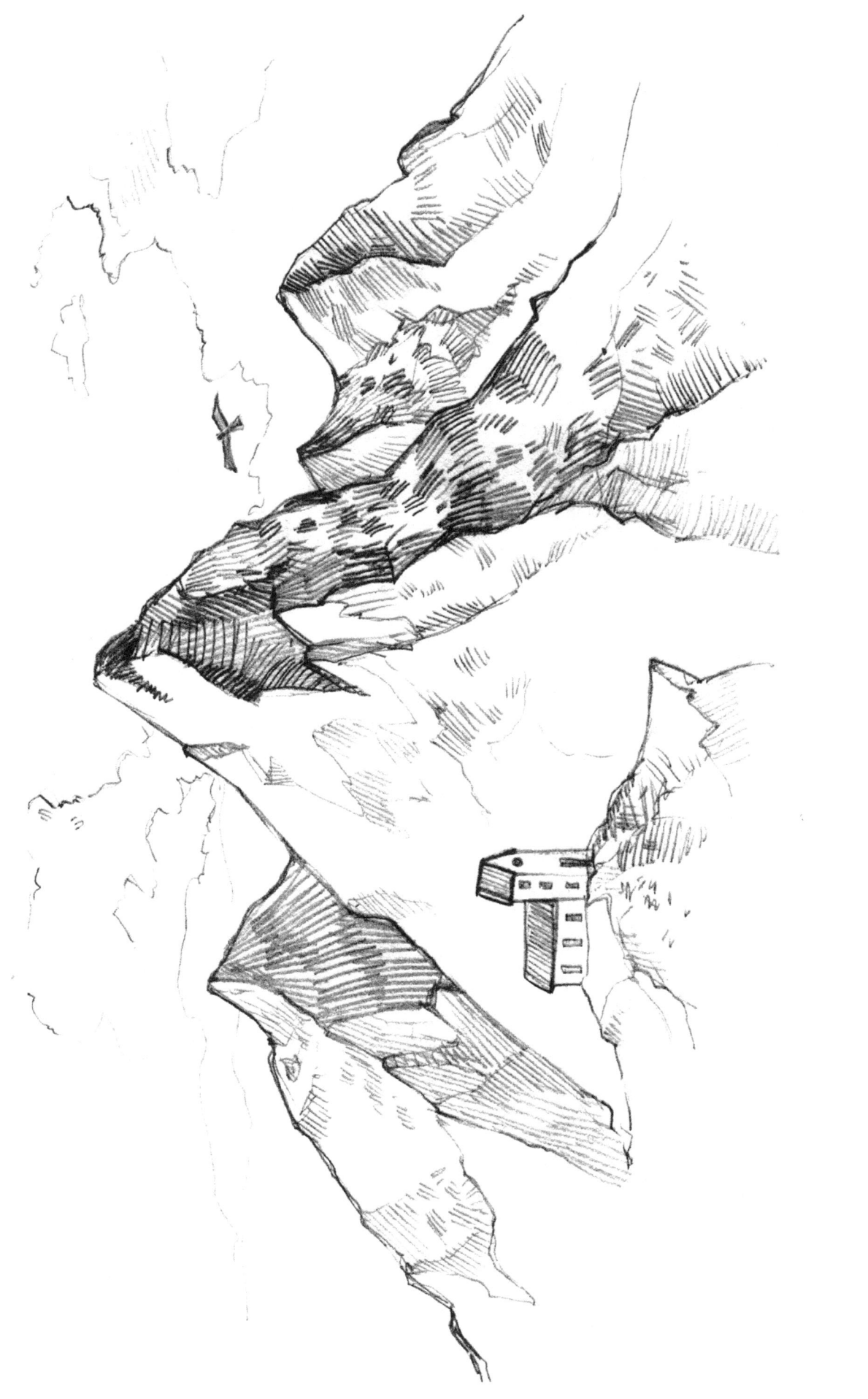

Thank you for coloring with us

More from our coloring books:

Seahorses
Coloring Book

Rachel Mintz

Thank you for coloring with us

Made in the USA
Coppell, TX
28 October 2020